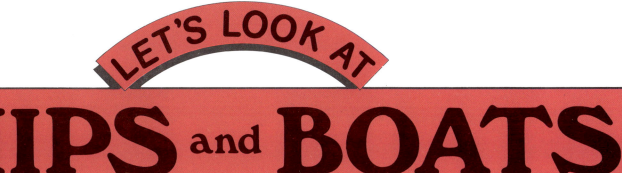

LET'S LOOK AT
SHIPS and BOATS

Rupert Matthews

Language consultant
Diana Bentley
University of Reading

Artist
Mike Atkinson

Let's Look At

Aircraft	Dinosaurs	Sharks
Bears	Farming	Ships and Boats
Big Cats	Horses	Sunshine
Bikes	Monster Machines	Tractors
Birds	Outer Space	Trains
Castles	Rain	Trucks
Circuses	Racing Cars	Volcanoes
Colours	The Seasons	Whales

Editors: Mike Hirst and Anna Girling

First published in 1989 by
Wayland (Publishers) Ltd
61 Western Road, Hove
East Sussex BN3 1JD, England

British Library Cataloguing in Publication Data
Matthews, Rupert
   Let's look at ships & boats.
   1. Boats & ships – For children
   I. Title II. Atkinson, Michael
   623.8'2

ISBN 1–85210–629–8

Phototypeset by Kalligraphics Ltd, Horley, Surrey
Printed and bound by Casterman, S.A., Belgium

Words printed in
bold are explained
in the glossary

Contents

On the water

Ships and boats carry people and goods across rivers, lakes or oceans. Some ships are very large. Other ships are quite small because they do not carry many people or goods.

Some people own small boats which they use for fun. They may sail them on lakes or the sea, or row them along rivers. All boats must be very well built. Then they can withstand storms or large waves without sinking.

Sail and oar

Most modern ships are driven by powerful engines, but in the past ships used sails or oars for movement. Two thousand years ago the Greeks and Romans used ships called **galleys**. Each galley was rowed by hundreds of men.

Until about 150 years ago all ships were powered by sail. Sailing ships called **clippers** carried tea between China and Europe. Clippers sailed very fast and often raced each other around the world.

The steamers

The first **steamers** were built about 160 years ago. They were the first ships with engines. Unlike sailing ships, steamships could move when there was no wind, or when the wind was blowing in the wrong direction.

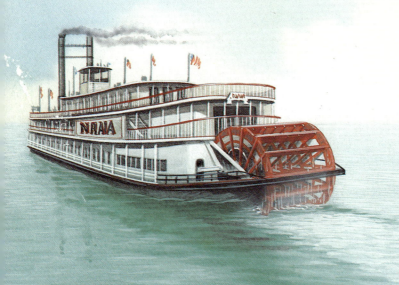

About 120 years ago the first steel ships were built. Steel is much stronger than wood and can be used for building large ships.

Merchant ships

Merchant ships carry goods such as motorcars, coal or food from one country to another. They sometimes have cranes on deck which help to load and unload goods on the ship.

Container ships are a new type of craft. They carry goods in large steel boxes called containers. These are lifted off the ship straight on to a lorry at the **dock**.

Harvesting the sea

Many types of fish, shellfish and other animals live in the sea. They can be caught by fishermen and are an important kind of food.

There are many kinds of fishing boats. Trawlers drag nets behind them. They catch fish, such as cod and plaice, which live at the bottom of the sea.

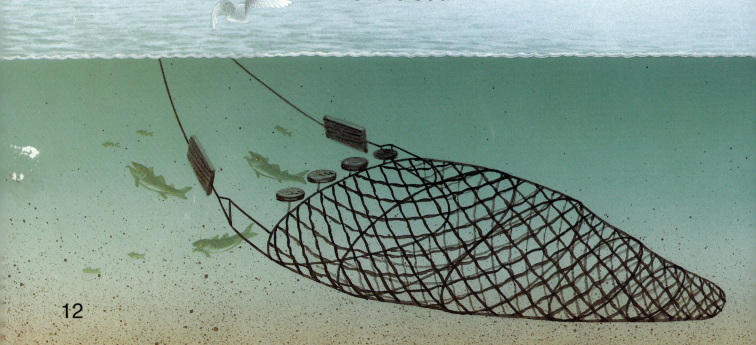

Other boats have purse seine nets. These nets make a loop and catch fish such as sardines and herring which live near the surface.

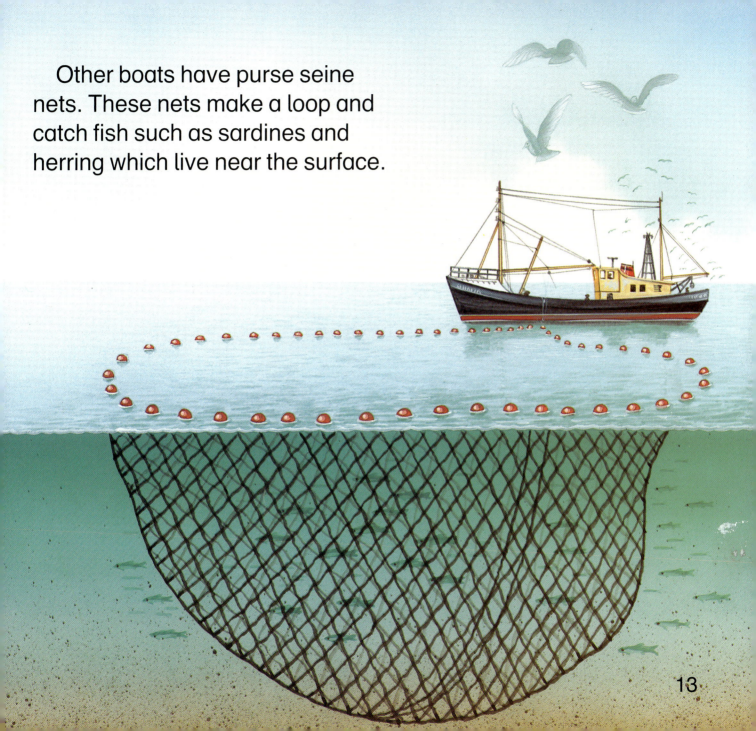

14

Passenger ships

Ships called car ferries take people and vehicles across short stretches of water, such as rivers and **straits**. These ferries have long flat **decks** where cars and lorries can park. The top decks have cafés and lounges for passengers.

Cruise liners carry people on holiday, calling at beautiful or historic **ports**. These ships are like floating hotels, with bedrooms, restaurants and swimming pools.

Ships with a special job

Many ships are built to do one special job. A research ship carries scientists and scientific instruments to study the ocean and sea life.

Icebreakers are very strong ships used in cold waters to smash surface ice so that other ships can pass through behind them.

Drilling ships have equipment which can drill into the seabed to search for oil or gas. Dredgers dig out the mud on the seabed to make the water deep enough for the larger ships.

To the rescue

Sometimes a ship is damaged or gets into trouble. It may hit rocks during a storm or it may catch fire. Then, lifeboats set out to rescue the ship. Lifeboatmen try to pass a **lifeline** to the sinking ship and rescue the people on board.

Warships

When countries go to war, they try to sink each other's ships. Many countries have warships which carry several different kinds of weapons.

An aircraft carrier can launch helicopters and planes against the enemy. Frigates are fast ships armed with guns and **missiles**. Submarines hide beneath the sea and fire **torpedoes** to sink the enemy's ships.

Boats for fun

Many boats are used for pleasure at sea. People who own sailing **yachts** often race against each other for fun. Powerboats are able to travel very quickly, faster than most racing cars. They take part in races, too.

Some people like to water-ski, being pulled behind motorboats. Other people are keen on the sport of windsurfing.

23

Lake, river and canal boats

Some people own small pleasure boats even if they do not live near the sea. They like to go sailing on rivers or lakes instead.

Some people enjoy sailing motor boats or holiday **barges**. They may sail up a river or canal to find a place for a picnic.

Traditional boats

In many parts of the world people continue to use traditional boats. These boats have been built in the same way for hundreds of years.

Junk

Junks are used on wide rivers in China and have sails made of bamboo. Small boats called dahabiahs carry passengers on the river Nile in Egypt. Many Chinese people live on board small boats called sampans.

Dahabiahs

Record-breaking ships

The largest ship ever built was the **tanker** *Seawise Giant*. It was 458 m long and weighed 564,800 tonnes. It was built in 1976 but was later destroyed in 1988.

The largest battleship ever built was the *Yamato*. It was 263 m long and weighed 73,000 tonnes. It was used by Japan during the Second World War until it was sunk in 1945.

The fastest powerboat in the world is the *Texan* which has travelled at a speed of 368 kph.

Yamato

Texan

Seawise Giant

Glossary

Barge   A boat with a flat bottom.

Clipper   A sailing ship once used to bring goods from China or Australia to Europe and America.

Deck   The floor of a ship.

Dock   A place where ships load and unload goods.

Galley   A large ship powered by oars.

Lifeline   A rope or wire along which people can escape from sinking ships.

Missile   A weapon fired from a ship. It can be steered in flight.

Port   A place on the coast which is sheltered from storms, where ships can rest in safety.

Steamer   A ship powered by a steam engine.

Strait   A narrow area of sea between two areas of land.

Tanker   A type of ship designed to carry liquids, such as oil.

Torpedo   A missile fired underwater from a submarine.

Yacht   A small sailing boat used for sport or pleasure.

Books to read

Ships of the High Seas,
 Erik Abranson
 (Peter Lowe, 1976)
*Observer's Book of
 Warships*, Hugh Cowin
 (Frederick Warne, 1987)
Observer's Book Of Ships,
 Frank Dodman (Frederick
 Warne, 1987)
Looking at Merchant Ships,
 Cliff Lines (Wayland,
 1984)
Looking at Submarines,
 Cliff Lines (Wayland, 1984)

Index